MW00366123

WE LIE DOWN IN HOPE

WE LIE DOWN IN HOPE

Selections from
John Donne's Meditations on
Sickness

JOHN J. POLLOCK, EDITOR

David C. Cook Publishing Co.

ELGIN, ILLINOIS—WESTON, ONTARIO
FULLERTON, CALIFORNIA

WE LIE DOWN IN HOPE
© 1977 David C. Cook Publishing Co.

All rights reserved. Except for brief excerpts for review purposes, no part of this book may be reproduced or used in any form without written permission from the publisher.

Published by David C. Cook Publishing Co., Elgin, IL 60120
Printed in the United States of America

ISBN 0-89191-095-6
LC 77-78505

IN THE WINTER of 1623, the English author John Donne experienced a sudden, devastating illness. His *Devotions upon Emergent Occasions* traces the development of that illness, recording his spiritual meditations and prayers to God, as he strove to discover some meaning to the suffering brought on by his disease. Donne recovered, and the following year published his *Devotions*, which, incredibly enough, he had written entirely during the period when he was most ill. The following are selections from those *Devotions*.

As yet God suspends me
between heaven and earth,
as a meteor.
I am not in heaven
because an earthly body impedes me,
and I am not in the earth
because a heavenly soul sustains me.

O *Lord, I am not weary of Thy pace,*
nor weary of mine own patience.
I provoke Thee not with a prayer,
not with a wish,
not with a hope,
to more haste than consists with Thy purpose,
nor look that any other thing
should have entered into Thy purpose
but Thy glory.
To hear Thy steps coming towards me
is the same comfort
as to see Thy face present with me.
Whether Thou do the work of a thousand years
in a day,
or extend the work of a day
to a thousand years,
as long as Thou workest,
it is light and comfort.

Everything is immediately done
which is done when Thou wouldst have it done.
Thy purpose terminates every action,
and what was done before that
is undone yet.

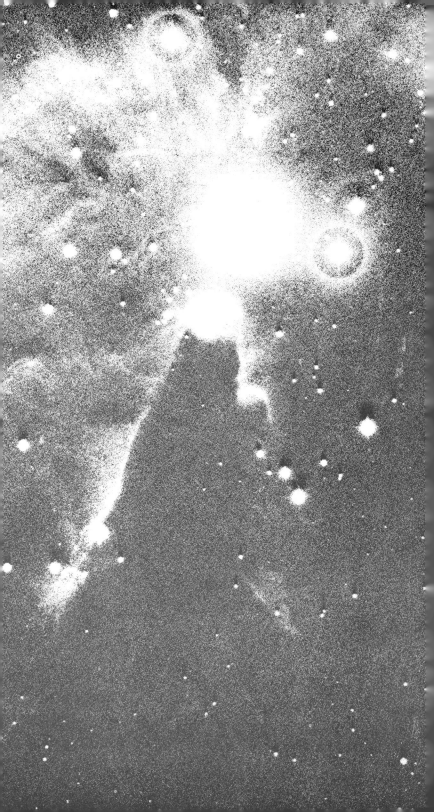

I say I wake, but my heart sleepeth;
my body is in a sick weariness,
but my soul in a peaceful rest with Thee.
And as our eyes in health
see not the air that is next to them,
nor the fire, nor the spheres,
nor stop upon anything till they come to stars,
so my eyes that are open
see nothing of this world,
but pass through all that and fix themselves
upon Thy peace and joy and glory above.

Our thoughts are our creatures,
creatures that are born giants,
that reach from East to West,
from Earth to Heaven,
that do not only bestride all the sea and land,
but span the sun and firmament at once.
My thoughts reach all,
comprehend all.
Inexplicable mystery:
I, their creator, am in a close prison,
in a sickbed, anywhere;
and any one of my creatures,
my thoughts,
is with the sun and beyond the sun,
overtakes the sun,
and overgoes the sun in one pace,
one step,
everywhere.

Earth is the center of my body;
heaven is the center of my soul.

I *know not what fear is,*
and I know not what it is that I fear now.
But my weakness is from nature,
who hath her measure;
my strength is from God,
Who possesses and distributes infinitely.
As my physician's fear
puts not him from his practice,
neither doth mine put me from receiving
from God and man and myself
spiritual and civil and moral assistances
and consolations.

Nay,
except there were some light,
there could be no shadow.

O *my God,*
Thou givest us fear for ballast
to carry us steadily in all weathers.
But Thou wouldst ballast us
with such sand as should have gold in it,
with that fear which is Thy fear,
for the fear of the Lord is His treasure.
He that hath that
lacks nothing that man can have,
nothing that God does give.

Joy includes all,
and fear and joy consist together,
nay, constitute one another.
Thy fear and Thy love are inseparable.
Give me, O Lord,
a fear of which I may not be afraid.

If I were but mere dust and ashes
I might speak unto the Lord,
for the Lord's hand made me of this dust,
and the Lord's hand shall re-collect these ashes;
the Lord's hand was the wheel
upon which this vessel of clay was framed,
and the Lord's hand is the urn
in which these ashes shall be preserved.
I am the dust and the ashes
of the temple of the Holy Ghost,
and what marble is so precious?
But I am more than dust and ashes:
I am my best part,
I am my soul.

When I asked, perchance, a stone,
He gave me bread;
when I asked, perchance, a scorpion,
He gave me a fish.

Therefore *am I cast down,*
that I might not be cast away.

The assurance of future mercy is present mercy.

Pray in thy bed at midnight,
and God will not say,
"I will hear thee tomorrow
upon thy knees at thy bedside."
Pray upon thy knees there then,
and God will not say,
"I will hear thee on Sunday at church."
God is no tardy God, no presumptuous God;
prayer is never unseasonable;
God is never asleep, nor absent.

He *that seeks Thee early*
shall receive Thy morning dew,
Thy seasonable mercy,
Thy forward consolation.

How little of a man is the heart,
and yet it is all by which he is.

I *know, O Lord, the discomfort*
that accompanies that phrase
"the house is visited
and Thy marks and Thy tokens are upon the patient";
but what a wretched and disconsolate hermitage
is that house which is not visited by Thee,
and what a waif and a stray
is that man that hath not Thy marks upon him?
These fevers, O Lord,
which Thou hast brought upon this body
are but Thy chafing of the wax,
that Thou mightest seal me to Thee;
these spots are but the letters
in which Thou hast written Thine own name
and conveyed Thyself to me.

We are God's tenants here,
and yet here He, our landlord,
pays us rents—
not yearly, nor quarterly,
but hourly and quarterly;
every minute He renews His mercy.

I must be poor and want,
before I can exercise the virtue of gratitude;
miserable and in torment,
before I can exercise the virtue of patience.

We cannot endure afflictions in ourselves, yet in Thee we can.

Only be Thou present to me,
O my God,
and this bedchamber and Thy bedchamber
shall be all one room,
and the closing of these bodily eyes here,
and the opening of the eyes of my soul there,
all one act.

As *Thou hast made this bed Thine altar,*
make me Thy sacrifice.

I *limit not,*
I condition not,
I choose not,
I wish not.

We lie down in a hope
that we shall rise the stronger.

Thou callest the dove
the "dove of the valleys,"
but promisest that the dove of the valleys
shall be upon the mountain.
As Thou hast laid me low in this valley of sickness,
so low that I am made fit for the question
asked in the field of bones,
"Son of man, can these bones live?"
so, in Thy good time,
carry me up to these mountains
of which even in this valley
Thou affordest me a prospect,
the mountain where Thou dwellest.

No man hath affliction enough
that is not matured and ripened by it
and made fit for God
by that affliction.

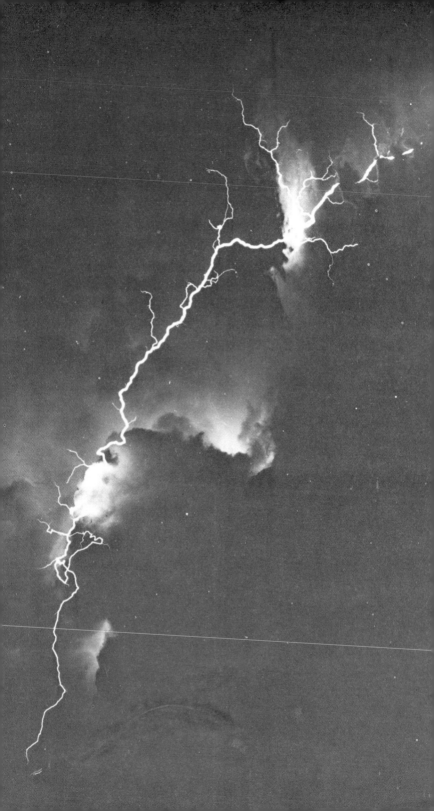

Tribulation
*is treasure in the nature of it,
but it is not
current money in the use of it
unless we get nearer
and nearer our home, heaven,
by it.*

Nature reaches out her hand
and gives us corn and wine and oil and milk;
but Thou fillest her hand before,
and Thou openest her hand
that she may rain down her showers upon us.
Industry reaches out her hand to us
and gives us fruits of our labor
for ourselves and our posterity;
but Thy hand guides that hand
when it sows and when it waters,
and the increase is from Thee.
Friends reach out their hands and prefer us;
but Thy hand
supports that hand that supports us.
Of all these Thy instruments
have I received Thy blessing, O God.

No man is an island,
entire of himself;
every man is a piece of the continent,
a part of the main.
If a clod be washed away by the sea,
Europe is the less,
as well as if a promontory were,
as well as if a manor of thy friends
or of thine own were.
Any man's death diminishes me,
because I am involved in mankind.
And therefore
never send to know for whom the bell tolls;
it tolls for thee.

The bell doth toll for him that thinks it doth;
and though it intermit again,
yet from that minute
that that occasion wrought upon him
he is united to God.
Who casts not up his eye
to the sun when it rises?
Who takes off his eye
from a comet when that breaks out?
Who bends not his ear
to any bell which upon any occasion rings?

All this while the physicians themselves
have been patients,
patiently attending
when they should see any land in this sea,
the maturity of the disease.
They must wait
till the season of the sickness come
and till it be ripened of itself,
and then they may put to their hand
to gather it before it fall off,
but they cannot hasten the ripening.

We cannot awake the July-flowers in January
nor retard the flowers of the spring to autumn.
We cannot bid the fruits come in May,
nor the leaves to stay on in December.

Thou, O God, art my strength,
and then what can be above it?
Mountains shake with the swelling of Thy sea;
men strong in grace are shaken with afflictions.
Even Thy corrections are of Thy treasure,
and Thou wilt not waste Thy corrections;
when they have done their service,
to humble Thy patient,
Thou wilt call them in again.

Thou art all.
Since Thou art so, O my God,
and affliction is a sea too deep for us,
what is our refuge?–
Thine ark,
Thy ship.

There are light hours enough
for any man to go his whole journey
intended by Thee.

To give
is an approaching to the condition of kings,
but to give health,
an approaching to the King of kings,
to Thee.
This assisting to my bodily health,
Thou knowest, O God,
is but the twilight of that day
wherein Thou hast shined upon me before,
but the echo of that voice
whereby Thou hast spoke to me before.

O *my God, my God,*
what thunder is not a well-tuned cymbal,
what hoarseness,
what harshness, is not a clear organ,
if Thou be pleased to set Thy voice to it?
And what organ is not well played on
if Thy hand be upon it?
Thy voice,
Thy hand, is in this sound,
and in this one sound
I hear the whole concert.

Since I find Thy whole hand light,
shall any finger of that hand
seem heavy?

To cure the sharp effects of diseases
is a great work;
to cure the disease itself
is a greater;
but to cure the body,
the root, the occasion of diseases,
is a work reserved for the Great Physician.

The power of grace is the strength of nature.

As he that would draw a circle on paper,
if he have brought that circle
within one inch of finishing
yet remove his compass,
he cannot make it up a perfect circle
unless he fall to work again
to find out the same center—
so, though setting that foot of my compass upon Thee,
I have gone far;
yet if I depart from Thee, my center,
all is imperfect.
This proceeding to action,
therefore, is a returning to Thee.

No man is well that understands not,
that values not,
his being well,
that hath not a cheerfulness and a joy in it.
And whosoever hath this joy
hath a desire to communicate,
to propagate that which occasions his happiness
and his joy to others.

PHOTO CREDITS

Grover Brinkman, page 10

Alan Cliburn, page 40

Camerique, page 26

A. Devaney, pages 16, 88

Ed Elsner, page 92

Rohn Engh, pages 28, 36, 46,
    58, 60, 80, 84, 90

HJM, pages 20, 54

Hedgecoth Photographers, page 24

Kaufmount Fabry, page 72

Harold M. Lambert, pages 34, 42, 62

Richard T. Lee, page 30

Jean-Claude Lejeune, page 56

Matson Photo Service, page 48

Robert Moust, page 64

Samuel Myslis, page 12

Religious News Service, pages 22, 50, 66

H. Armstrong Roberts, pages 8, 14, 18,
    32, 44, 52, 68, 70, 76, 82

Rick Smolen, page 86

Jim Whitmer, pages 38, 74